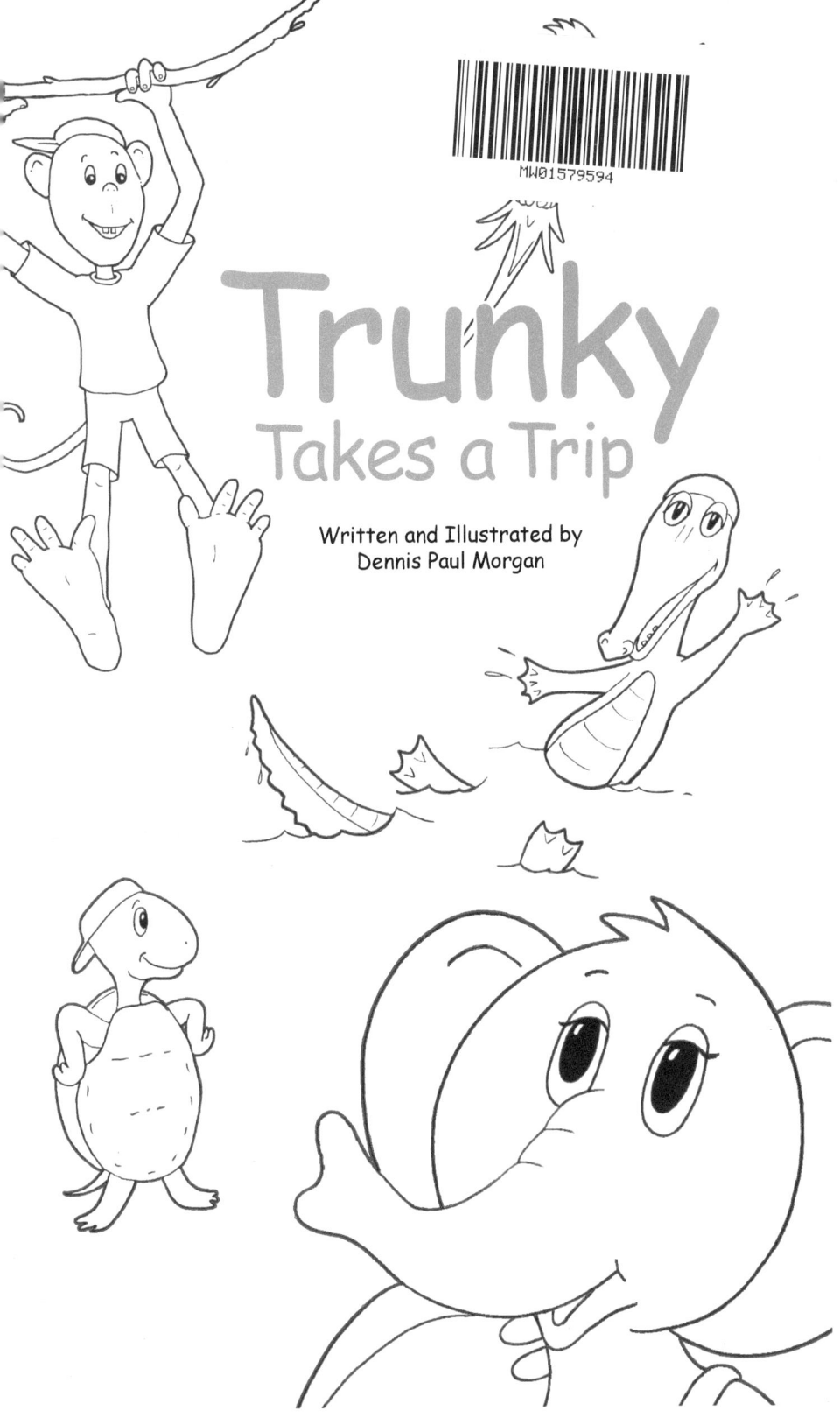

Thanks to Kathy, Amy, Matthew, and Breanna.
To my grandkids Penelope, Eleanor, Harvey, and Kirby.
To all my family, and friends.

Copyright © 2023 by Dennis Paul Morgan

All rights reserved.

No part of this publication may be reproduced, distributed, or transmitted in any form or by any means, including photocopying, recording, or other electronic or mechanical methods, without the prior written permission of the publisher, except as permitted by U.S. copyright law. For permission requests, contact Dennis Paul Morgan dpmorgan230@gmail.com

Written by Dennis Paul Morgan
Book Cover by Dennis Paul Morgan
Illustrations by Dennis Paul Morgan

First printed edition 2023
First video version 2010
https://youtu.be/BwczozwGQOA

Trunky
Takes a Trip

Written and Illustrated by
Dennis Paul Morgan

This is a little story of an elephant named Trunky. He lived with his family in the warm grasslands of Africa.

One day Trunky announced, "I want to go out on my own and visit the jungle."

His parents were very concerned and said, "Trunky you can't go to the jungle. It is very dank, dark and dangerous there."

But Trunky insisted and persisted until they gave in and let him go.

"Be careful, cautious and courteous son," said his mother and father. "REMEMBER to call us when you get there!"

Trunky knew he would REMEMBER because an elephant never, ever, at no time, no way, not once, NOT EVER FORGETS!

After many days of travel, Trunky arrived at the jungle. The first animal he met was a parrot.

"Hi bird. What's your name?" said Trunky.

"I'm not a bird. I'm a parrot," said the bird.

"I'm an elephant, and my name is Trunky."

"Nice to meet you, Trunky. I'm Spunky. Would you like to play?"

"But of course," said Trunky.

"Great," said Spunky. "Let's fly way up in the sky and soar above the treetops."

"I can't fly," said Trunky. "I haven't any wings."

"YOU CAN'T FLY? How can I play with you if you can't fly?" said Spunky as he flittered and fluttered away.

Left alone, Trunky continued his journey.

Next, Trunky met a monkey.

"Hi, my name is Trunky. What's yours?"

"The name's Funky, and I'm a monkey," said the monkey to Trunky.

"Would you like to play?" asked Trunky.

"Sure," said Funky the monkey. "Let's climb these trees and swing from limb to limb. It's a blast."

I can't climb a tree or swing on branches," said Trunky to Funky the monkey. "I haven't any thumbs."

"WHAT, not even on your feet? I can't hang around you if you can't climb," said Funky to Trunky and away he swung.

Alone again, Trunky moved on.

Soon he came upon another creature.

"Hello there, you in the water.
My name is Trunky."

"Hi, Trunky. I'm Chunky the crocodile.
Would you like to come in for a swim?"

"I would like to swim, but I can't. My tail is too small, and my feet are not webbed," replied Trunky.

"How strange," said Chunky. "Then I will be off." And away he swam.

Once again, Trunky was alone.

"Maybe my parents were right. I don't belong here. I don't fit in. I'm just an ordinary, little-bit-hairy, pachyderm."

"I SHOULD CALL and tell them I'm coming home."

Feeling rejected, Trunky neglected to look where he was walking.

"HEY, WATCH IT! You almost stepped on me!"

"Oh, I'm sorry. I thought you were a rock," said Trunky.

"A ROCK! Haven't you ever seen a tortoise before?"

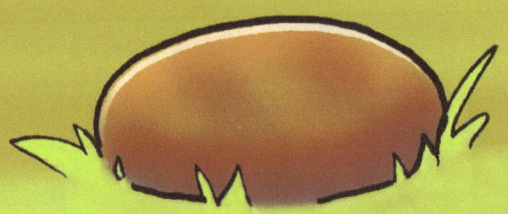

"No," said Trunky. "Sorry to disturb you."

"That's OK; happens all the time. I'm Punky," said the tortoise. "Would you like to play with me?"

"Hi Punky. I'm Trunky. I'm not much fun. I can't do anything. I can't fly. I can't climb. I can't even swim!"

"Well, I can't either, Trunky," said Punky.

"Doesn't that bother you, Punky?" said Trunky.

"Nope! My shell makes me special. It's my home away from home. It protects me, keeps me dry, and you should see it shine when I wax it."

"There's nothing special about me," said Trunky to Punky. "I'll just take my gray, wrinkled, slow, big-eared self and be going."

"WAIT!" said Punky. "There must be something about you that's special."

"I'm afraid not," said Trunky wiping a tear away with his trunk.

"I KNOW, I KNOW!" said Punky.

"You know what," said Trunky.

"I KNOW! YOUR NOSE! Your nose is noteworthy! How many creatures can wipe their eyes with their nose?" said Punky to Trunky.

"I guess I never noticed my nose. You know, I can pick things up with it, feed myself with it, breath through it, and play it like a trumpet. Now I know my nose makes me special after all."

"EVERYONE IS SPECIAL IN THEIR OWN WAY!" said Trunky.

"Will you stay and play with me?" asked Punky.

"YOU GOT IT!" said Trunky. "But first I have to do something. Something an elephant never, ever, at no time, no way, not once, NOT EVER DOES! "

"What's that, Trunky?"

Printed in the USA
CPSIA information can be obtained
at www.ICGtesting.com
LVHW071456300923
759797LV00001B/10